Exploring Justice: The Ten Commandments

—— VOLUME I ——

Leader's Guide

PRIORITIES

ANNE ROBERTSON

Copyright © 2019 by the Massachusetts Bible Society

All rights reserved. No part of this book may be reproduced, stored in a retrieval system, or transmitted in any form or by any means, electronic, mechanical, including photocopying, recording, or otherwise, without the written permission of the publisher.

Unless otherwise indicated, Bible quotations in this book are from the New Revised Standard Version Bible, copyright © 1989 by the National Council of Churches of Christ in the U.S.A. Used by permission. All rights reserved.

Massachusetts Bible Society
831 Beacon St. #324
Newton Center, MA 02459

Book design by Thomas Bergeron
www.thomasbergeron.com
Typeface: Garamond, Gill Sans

ISBN-13: 978-1-7338360-0-5
1st Edition

To Bill and Joan Humphrey
whose lives display
God's priorities at work in the world

CONTENTS

- 7 **Welcome**
  - 7 What Is this Exactly?
  - 8 Confessions of a Biased Author

- 9 **You, Leader, Have One Job**

- 12 **Session Elements and Their Objectives**
  - 12 In One Voice
  - 13 Check-In
  - 13 Discussion Questions
  - 13 Exercises

- 14 **Becoming an Effective Small Group Leader**
  - 14 Tricks of the Trade
  - 16 Leader, Know Thyself
  - 17 Tips for Avoiding Small Group Headaches
  - 17 Elements of a Good Learning Space for Small Groups

- **Lesson Plans**
  - 19 Session One: Priorities: The Path to Justice
  - 31 Session Two: Pretenders: How to Spot an Idol
  - 39 Session Three: Allegiance: How Idols Confuse Our Priorities
  - 49 Session Four: Supremacy: How Idols Divide Us
  - 61 Session Five: Freedom: The Bulwark Against Idolatry
  - 71 Session Six: Armed: How to Tame Your Idol

- **Handouts**
  - 81 Social Justice Bingo
  - 83 Imagining Justice
  - 85 Beyond the Bend—A Parable
  - 87 Cantwell v. Connecticut

- **Other**
  - 89 "In One Voice"
  - 91 Group Covenant Template
  - 93 Exploring Justice Final Evaluation—Leader
  - 95 Exploring Justice Final Evaluation—Student
  - 97 Advertising Helps

WELCOME

WHAT IS THIS EXACTLY?

You may know the Massachusetts Bible Society from our popular Bible study series, *Exploring the Bible: The Dickinson Series*. You may know me, Anne Robertson, for a variety of sermons and books on religion and the Bible. This book is both like and unlike what I've written in the past. The focus of this study series is on issues of justice in the public square. The Bible is the lens through which we are examining those issues, but, just as with reading glasses, the biblical lens will often fade into the periphery as it does its job of helping us see what's on the page. Here are a few important things to know before you dig in:

- **It's a series, designed to be read in order.** *Exploring Justice: The Ten Commandments* is a multi-volume series, and you are holding just one of its volumes. If this is your first encounter with this series and you're not looking at Volume 1, you will be at a disadvantage.

If this is your first encounter with this series and you're not looking at Volume 1, you will be at a disadvantage.

Starting with the command to have no other gods, each volume of *Exploring Justice* covers between one and three different commandments. The first volume establishes core themes that flow throughout the entire series, and each subsequent volume builds on that, just as the Ten Commandments themselves build on one another. Lightning will not strike if you do them out of order, but you will be quite likely to misunderstand or struggle. If you're joining a group that has already done another volume, at least pick up a copy of any volumes you may have missed and read the student book.

- **"Bible study" isn't exactly the right way to describe this series.** You will encounter the Bible in this study and, as the series title implies, the whole premise is that the Ten Commandments can help us keep today's social issues in conversation with the timeless values that inform our faith. You will also consider other passages from both the Old and New Testaments that relate to the themes of each chapter, and you'll be asked to think about their relevance to the issues at hand. In a typical Bible study, however, the object of study is the Bible itself, which is not the case here.

- **A Christian audience is assumed but not necessary.** Most of the people who do this study will be Christians in churches, but we ran a pilot group of humanists in a Unitarian congregation who also found it helpful. It's our hope that interfaith groups might also find the series useful for dialogue and understanding.

The Ten Commandments themselves are presented in the context of faith in the God of Abraham, Isaac, and Jacob, and they offer covenant relationship with that God. But, as a legal code, the commandments provide many points of connection to other religions as well as to contemporary, secular life. No matter our faith or lack thereof, we each have our own lens for viewing justice, and our own ideas of what values should be prioritized in society.

All of us will be looking at the teachings of the Bible and deciding whether the wisdom found there has anything to say to a given issue. Christians will have a different view of the authority of those teachings, but there's plenty of old-fashioned wisdom in the Bible that can shed light on our struggles, even for those who don't profess to "believe" it in the way that Christians do.

- **You can learn, even if everyone agrees.** This is a series about you, not those who disagree with you. It is designed to help you look inward at your own engagement with justice issues, not to encourage finger-pointing at those who reach different conclusions. While group discussions are enhanced by a diversity of people and opinions, there is much that we can learn about ourselves even within a group that is otherwise like-minded and from a similar background. This study will help you reflect not just on particular issues, but on the way we approach discussing those issues with others. It's possible to be "right" on any given issue and still violate our values in the way we approach others who hold a different position.

It's possible to be "right" on any given issue and still violate our values in the way we approach others who hold a different position.

- Jesus scolded those who tried to take a speck out of the eye of someone else while ignoring the logs in their own eyes, and this series tries to take that to heart. Bring a mirror to your study rather than one of those pointing foam fingers. If you look deeply and honestly into your own heart, you will also be much better equipped to handle any actual diversity in your group. You'll be so busy looking at the root of your own opinions and behavior that you'll be less likely to respond in a judgmental way to others.

> **Thank You for Supporting Us**
>
> Like our *Exploring the Bible* series, 100 percent of sales revenue from this series supports the mission of the historic Massachusetts Bible Society, a 501(c)3 charitable organization that exists to promote biblical literacy, understanding, and dialogue. You can learn more about the series and its other volumes by visiting us at massbible.org/exploring-justice. We are now in our third century, thanks to supporters who buy our books and/or make donations. If you'd like to help us even more, visit massbible.org/support-us.

CONFESSIONS OF A BIASED AUTHOR

Exploring Justice: The Ten Commandments wasn't written by a bot. It wasn't even written by a team of people. It was written by a single human—in this case, me. While I have done my best to be fair in presenting the issues, I have my own beliefs, ideas, and opinions about each topic in the book—just as every reader will—and it's probably a pipe dream to think that my own bias won't come through here and there.

So, I'll make a deal with you. As we go along, I'll poke my head out from time to time to share experiences or opinions on the subject at hand. I won't hide behind the voice of a supposedly impartial narrator, except when it comes to relating history or other factual information that you can look up and check yourself. You will know where I stand, which allows you to argue back in your group sessions instead of shadow boxing. In my own sharing, I'll try to model a way to express opinions and experiences that helps make real listening and dialogue possible. In return, I will ask that each of you do the same with your group, or, if you're just reading on your own, with whomever you choose to talk to about any of these issues. If you find I haven't done that, feel free to blast me in the evaluation at the end of this volume—tactfully, of course. Therapy is expensive.

I am the executive director of the Massachusetts Bible Society, and it's fair to say that they wouldn't publish this if they thought it was heresy. Both staff and board members were part of our pilot groups. But the opinions you'll find throughout these volumes are my own and have not received formal endorsement from the MBS board, members, or partner organizations. You can find the organization's official statement on Scripture at massbible.org/about-us/mission-statement.

YOU, LEADER, HAVE ONE JOB

The following is true about all small group leaders, but it is doubly true for those leading Exploring Justice: The Ten Commandments: The most successful leaders are those with well-developed people skills. You don't have to be the smartest person or the bravest person or the "best" at anything in particular to lead this study. You can learn and think and grow right along with your group. But, if you want your group to be successful, you will have to focus like a laser on one thing: Keeping everyone engaged in respectful dialogue. Let's look at what every word of that means.

Keeping. You are the keeper of the group, which is to say that you are a steward. Do not undervalue the trust that is being placed in you when people sign up to talk about issues that are shaking faith and culture and, in most cases, have shaken it for a hundred years or more. There are few places that people can turn to better understand what keeps us so roiled up and to safely express their views and questions. Those who have signed up for this course have decided that this group might be such a place; your job is to make sure that they find it.

That steward's role doesn't require perfection—none of us ever gets it completely right—but it does require that if we get it wrong, we take responsibility and apologize. In doing so, we model for the group the kind of behavior that makes any place safe for difficult discussions and encourages others to do the same. This group is not a battle for you to win; it is a garden for you to tend. But what if you have really difficult people in your group? We'll get to that, but the first concern in any kind of group is to make sure that you, dear Leader, are not that difficult person!

Everyone. It may seem that your group is moving along nicely. The dialogue is interesting, differences don't cause division, and everything seems fine. That's good as far as it goes, but your job is to make sure that everyone's voice is being heard. It could be that the reason everyone is so agreeable is because those with differing views are unable or unwilling to express them. While leaders should never force people to share, and anyone can have an off day when they'd rather just be quiet, if anyone in your group consistently says little to nothing, you have an issue. The group is being deprived of an important voice.

The solution will depend on why a person is not engaging. Before we talk about those possible reasons and their remedies, let's be clear that leaders should never, ever inquire about those reasons publicly. "Hey, Joan, why not speak up? Cat got your tongue?" "Marcus, why don't you ever say anything? Are we that scary?" That person will leave and never come back. If you happen to know the person, you may already have some insight into why he or she may be so quiet; if you don't, there are a few things you can try out to get a better understanding of the issue.

Or, you can talk to the person privately and say something like, "I'm so glad you're part of this group. You don't say much when we meet, so I feel like we're missing out on your perspective. Is there something I could do as the leader to give you more of an opportunity to speak? There's no pressure—if you're happy; I'm happy. But I wanted you to know that I value your voice, and if there's a way I can help support you, then I'd like to know."

One reason can be a simple matter of personality. Some people eagerly talk before a group of ten or twenty people; others simply will not open up to a group that large, even if they've known everyone a long time. In several places this material suggests that you subdivide your group into two or more smaller groups. Many groups resist this—especially those who already know each other well—and if everyone in your group regularly shares their thoughts, you're fine to keep it that way. But if you have even a single person who regularly says nothing, consider the possibility that you might need at least one opportunity in each session for discussion in smaller groups.

Another personality-driven issue has more to do with the other personalities in the group. Do you have one or two people who always have a lot to say? The extroverts will jump into a discussion feet first, and frequently figure out what they want to say by talking it out. That can leave those who need time to think before speaking, out of the discussion. By the time they know what they want to say, the conversation has moved on. On p. 14 you can read about the "talking stick," a way to make sure that extroverts don't drive the train out of the station before everyone has had a chance to board. There are some exercises that explicitly direct you to use a talking stick of some kind, but some leaders find it useful all the time. As long as you explain what it's for and use it consistently, it's not a controversial tool.

It's also possible that someone is not speaking up because they believe—rightly or wrongly—that their voice is unwelcome. Maybe their opinion on an issue is different from the majority in the group—or maybe it's only different from one dominant group member who has slapped them down or judged them in the past. In this case, your job is to be like the icebreaker ships in the Arctic—clear a path for that person's views.

Especially if the bulk of the group is of one opinion and no one is expressing a different point of view, you can clear a path for the dissenters by saying something like, "Everyone seems to be basically on the same page on this, so let's think for a minute about where those who might differ are coming from. If you were assigned to debate this issue from the other side, what would be your arguments?" You can do something similar based on the reading: "Did the reading about this issue seem balanced to you? Were there perspectives the author left out?"

But the most important way you can clear a path for a variety of views is to enforce the group covenant that you'll establish in your first session. If someone speaks up and someone else slaps them down, the covenant allows you to step in publicly without it being seen as a personal attack. Step in immediately with something like, "There are strong emotions around these issues, but let's remember our group covenant and our promise to be respectful toward one another. We're all in this together." If necessary, use the candle technique described on p. 15 and invite people to take a moment of silence and focus on the flame before returning to the discussion. If someone repeatedly violates the covenant, you'll need to ask that person—privately—to leave the group. See p. 17 for more on this.

Engaged. Just because a person is speaking does not mean that they are engaged. Sometimes people like to throw bombs into a discussion to turn a healthy debate into a divisive one. Others really like to talk about something that's off-topic and get the group off track and onto an unrelated subject. Even without someone actively trying to thwart a discussion, the topics you'll be dealing with almost always overlap with other equally significant issues and it can be easy for a group to drift.

Your job as a leader is not only to make sure all voices are heard, but also to ensure that the larger conversation is relevant to the subject at hand. In each session you will find objectives, both for the group session as a whole and for each individual exercise. Your task is to keep an eye on those objectives and make sure your group is at least in the neighborhood of those goals.

For example, in many sessions you have a block of thirty minutes for general discussion of the reading. Those discussion times give you a list of questions to get discussion started. The objective for that thirty minutes is not to ask every one of those questions—or even any of those questions. It's to discuss the topics presented in the reading that was done for homework. If you need one or more of those questions to get things going, or if you find one or more of them interesting, by all means use them. But if you've got a discussion of the reading going on, you don't have to stop an interesting debate just to get to the next question on the list. In almost no case would you have time to fully discuss every question in thirty minutes anyway. The objectives let you know that as long as you're discussing the reading, you're good. Use questions that are helpful to meet that goal; skip ones that don't.

With the objectives to guide you, you have a way to bring back a wayward discussion while avoiding the appearance of a personal attack on the person responsible for the tangent. You can simply say something like, "This is really interesting, but my job is to make sure we cover the objective for this exercise, which says... ." Then you can use one of the discussion questions to get back on track. The objectives aren't secret; there's no reason you can't share them with your group. In fact, if the group seems confused about why they're being asked to do something, sharing the objective might help.

Respectful. The reason this series exists is because in our U.S. culture, we've become increasingly unable to engage in respectful dialogue, and sometimes it seems like the church is the worst offender. "I don't need to be politically correct" has become a way of saying, "I don't need to respect you when I speak." This series takes seriously the claim of 1 John 4:8 that "God is love," while 1 Corinthians 13:4–5 reminds us that "love is patient; love is kind; love is not envious or boastful or arrogant or rude. It does not insist on its own way; it is not irritable or resentful." Embodying that is the goal for your group.

Your purpose is not to get everyone to agree about an issue. If people come in with different positions and leave with different positions, your group has not failed. This is about unity, not uniformity. The most successful groups will be those whose members are able to listen to and therefore better understand those whose ideas differ from their own. In a successful group, strongly held opinions will be approached with curiosity rather than fear. Your members will express this curiosity with words like these: "I hear what you're saying, but I don't understand it. Can you help me understand where you're coming from? I want to learn."

Don't worry: We haven't left you on your own. The exercises you'll find here, and progression of the chapters in this material, are all designed to help groups foster respectful conversation, especially by focusing on the history behind some of the symbols, ideas, and rhetoric we all use without much thought or understanding. But none of that will matter if a respectful tone isn't maintained, and that's true even if everyone in the group is of the same mind. While you certainly should never let one group member be disrespected by another, it's also your job to make sure that a group of like-minded people doesn't speak disrespectfully of others—even if they're not present. Of course you can strongly disagree with positions, but the trick to being respectful is separating the position from the person who holds it. That is love-your-enemies hard—but it's how we all move forward together.

If your group struggles with this, I would suggest a discussion with a prison chaplain or someone else engaged in prison ministry. People who do that work have to come to a place where they can love and serve people who have done some of the worst things people can do to one another. They have learned that justice doesn't mean stomping out the people working against our interests. It doesn't mean more for me and less for you. It means understanding why people believe as they do, seeing our own human struggles in them, and finding a way where everyone—rather than just one side—gets justice in all its fullness.

Dialogue. If you've kept everyone engaged respectfully, dialogue—real dialogue—will be the natural result. These studies are not designed as lectures. As the group leader, you will give instructions, jump in to keep time on an exercise, and generally help keep a conversation going. But you should not be the "teacher" in the usual sense of that word. You do not need to be the expert imparting information. You are a facilitator, guiding a group through exercises designed to produce constructive conversation. Notice that the goal is not solutions to the issues we'll be talking about. We need solutions to be sure, but this series isn't designed to provide them. It's designed to help us practice the honest and respectful dialogue that is needed to reach those solutions. And you're the leader who will help guide your group to that goal.

SESSION ELEMENTS AND THEIR OBJECTIVES

IN ONE VOICE

From monks and yogis to sports teams and armies; from church choirs to Jewish cantors to the call to prayer from the minaret of a mosque, civilizations have long understood the role that music plays in bringing people together and uniting them for a common purpose. Because the topics raised in every volume of this series are contentious, the plan for each session will include time to begin and end with a song. This material is designed to help turn down the temperature enough for real listening, understanding, and dialogue to occur. Music, especially singing together, has the power to do that. Here's how it works.

At the beginning and end of every session will be a very short element called "In One Voice" which will ask you to sing a song in unison. In the back of this guide on p. 89 are some suggestions for those elements, or you might have something else that is not on the list. Keep the following things in mind when making your choice:

1. Whatever you select for each position (beginning and ending), keep it the same for every session. By letting it become routine, participants can relax and let it be a harbor of safe return when emotions and anxiety may run high. You might even decide you want to use the same thing in both places every week. It's up to you. But don't keep mixing it up. Use the same opening and the same closing every single time.

2. Sing in unison. Harmony is fine and even a round, but no solos, duets, or other things that can be interpreted as a performance, except for when you are first teaching the song. Everyone should join in if they are physically able to do so, even if they can't carry a tune in a bucket. If someone is unable to speak or sing, have them mouth the words, direct with their arms, or tap the beat on the edge of a table. Find a way to include everyone. Make sure the song is easily sung by a group. There are lots of great songs out there that are wonderful when we hear them performed but that are very difficult for a random group of untrained singers to sing together.

3. Select songs that are uplifting and focused on unity. This is not the time for confession of sin, facing a challenge, arousing patriotism, or gearing up for a fight. Those things will all come up during the reading, discussions, and exercises. This is a chance for participants to pull back and find their center, to be reassured of their value, and to connect to others in a way that is at once less direct and more powerful. Praise songs are fine as long as you don't have an interfaith group or participants who might not share the sentiment of the song.

4. Think about the tempo of the song you select. A rousing, upbeat song will raise energy levels, while a slower, almost chant-like song can calm those who are prone to anger or are easily upset. If the personalities in your group are anxious about the study and somewhat wary of speaking their minds, then an upbeat song can give them confidence. If you have a group with strong personalities that are eager to jump into the fray, you may want to pick a more soothing song to keep the temperature at a manageable level.

5. Keep them short: A refrain from a hymn, a benediction, a single stanza. If you want something longer, then break it up across the two segments. Just keep it the same from week to week, do it together, and make it peaceful. You might also consider lighting a candle during the opening. See p. 15 in this introduction for more on that practice.

6. If your group absolutely rebels against singing, then have them speak something in unison. That could be the lyrics to a song, a meaningful poem or prayer, or some other affirmation. Do not read it to them.

Let all voices join together somehow—preferably in song, but speaking together is also an option. The Prayer of St. Francis is a good option here.

7. Whatever you pick can be another tool in your toolbox if a given discussion is starting to get overheated or if people are shutting down. There are more of these in the "Tricks of the Trade" section on p. 14, but you can also simply pause a discussion at any time during your session and return to your song to help reset the mood.

CHECK-IN

Beginning in session two, each group session begins with a set of two Check-In questions about the material covered in that session:

- What is one thing that was new to me in this material?
- What is one question that this week's topic(s) raises for me?

These questions are posed in the student book to help participants prepare for the next group, so ideally they have already thought about them and have written a response to each in their own books. These are not designed to be discussion questions. Responses should be one or two sentences at most, simply stated by participants without any elaboration. The questions serve to focus the group on the topic and allow the leader to gauge where students are. They also allow participants to hear, from others, questions or issues they may not have thought about themselves.

DISCUSSION QUESTIONS

In addition to discussion questions that might be part of an exercise, several sessions have a half-hour block devoted to discussion of the week's reading. The questions provided in this guide are to help you generate discussion. It is fine if you have your own set of questions or if there are things that come up in the Check-In that the group would like to explore in this next section. If a particular question falls flat with your group, you can try rephrasing it in your own words, giving some examples, or just moving on to a different question. Not every question will resonate with every group.

But also try not to panic in an initial silence. It can take a minute for people to process a question and think of how they want to respond. Some groups can benefit from an intentional moment of silence between asking a question and letting someone make the first response. Lastly, there is no need to get through every question on a given list. As long as the group is discussing the reading and remains engaged, it's fine. It is better to have a meaningful discussion about two questions than it is to rush through ten just for the sake of asking them all.

EXERCISES

Each session has at least one block that is a more structured activity. The additional structure is designed to help a group navigate the difficult issues being discussed with respect and care. The last portion of each chapter in the student book introduces the topic, provides history and context, and asks participants to reflect on the questions that will inform the structured exercises when they meet. No one who has done the homework should come to these topics cold. Periodically, remind the group that if they are unable to do all the reading for a given session, they should at least try to read through that final section of each chapter so that they can fully engage with the group.

You will not have time to fully explore any one of the topics in these exercises. They are all huge topics that have many layers and that have challenged us for years, decades, or even centuries. You won't resolve them in a thirty or forty-five minute exercise. This may frustrate you or others in the group who are problem-solvers. You can help that frustration by managing expectations and helping the group to realize that, in our polarized culture, just being able to talk about a difficult issue without rancor for a half hour is progress. If you manage to create a place where those with differing opinions feel heard and respected, you have opened the door that leads toward justice.

BECOMING AN EFFECTIVE SMALL GROUP LEADER

These next few sections will certainly help you to lead this series, but they're also reliable tips for leading a small group of any kind.

TRICKS OF THE TRADE: DIFFUSING DIFFICULT SITUATIONS

Those leading a group for the first time are often worried about their ability to rein in a group that has gone rogue in one way or another. Our worst fears rarely come to pass, and they are even less likely to happen if we keep just a few tools handy. Here are four common strategies, several of which will be suggested in the exercises for this study.

The Parking Lot

Q: What is it?

A: A (usually large) piece of paper where you can write questions or issues.

Q: When do you need it?

A: When someone has a question or concern that is somewhat related to the topic, but you can't stop to talk about it right then.

Q: What do you say?

A: "That's a great question! While we can't stop to talk about it right now, I'm going to put it here in the parking lot so we don't forget it. If it doesn't get addressed by later discussions, we'll come back to it."

Q: What do you do?

A: Write it down and don't lose it. Preferably you write it on something large enough that everyone can see that you did indeed write the question. If it gets dealt with in the regular course of things, cross it off the list. If not, make a time to address it either in a group session or privately with the person who expressed the concern.

Q: Why does it work?

A: Assuming it was a sincere question and not an attempt to divert the group, the person feels validated because their question/comment was taken seriously. It helps the questioner feel good, and it helps the group stay on track: Win/win—unless you never actually deal with the parking lot questions. In that case people will learn not to trust you and you will lose effectiveness as a leader.

The Talking Stick

Q: What is it?

A: A stick or some other hand-held object that can be passed from person to person when it's their turn to talk.

Q: When do you need it?

A: If you have one or more people who like to talk a lot, who interrupt others frequently, or who tend to dominate conversations.

Q: What do you say?

A: "I've noticed that some of our quieter members sometimes have trouble jumping into a lively conversation, so we're going to try using this talking stick. Only the person with the stick gets to speak. I'll make sure the stick gets around so that everyone who wants to speak has a chance."

Q: What do you do?

A: Figure out your own system of "stick management." You could have people raise their hands to get the stick or you might just sense someone wanting to get into the conversation. If you are passing the stick around the room, make sure people have permission to take it and simply say "pass" before handing it to the next person. Forcing someone to speak when they don't want to can be just as damaging as never giving them the opportunity to speak in the first place. You may also have to gently take the stick from someone who just won't quit talking. Think cueing the music for someone accepting an Oscar.

Q: Why does it work?

A: Often, those who dominate conversations aren't trying to be difficult. Many are just extroverts who are really engaged in the topic. The talking stick is something everyone can see, with rules that everyone can understand. When you use it, you will have fewer interruptions, more participation, and the assurance that all who wish to share have been able to do so.

Lighting a Candle

Q: What is it?

A: A lit candle, usually in the center of the group or at the front. Don't use scented candles—someone will have an allergy. Make sure the candle is large enough to burn for the length of your session. Battery-powered candles are getting nicer all the time and are always an option.

Q: When do you need it?

A: Candles are soothing, so if you are dealing with topics where debate could be heated or just with personalities that could use a bit of soothing, having a candle lit is always helpful. Since a heated debate can sometimes seem to come out of nowhere, just having one as a matter of course doesn't hurt.

Q: What do you say?

A: "I think we could use a slight pause here to gather our thoughts. Just sit for a moment, focus on the light of the candle and take some deep breaths. Then we can move to the next topic." (Or you may continue or begin a new activity.)

Q: What do you do?

A: Exactly what you told the group you'd do—maintain a quiet pause. Time it for a minute or two and then re-engage the group in whatever way seems best. You could return to the discussion after everyone has calmed down a bit or move on to another topic. If you typically have a break in your sessions, take the break after the candle focus. If you go directly to a break to end an overheated debate, your group will fracture into sides during the break and some might leave. If a discussion has escalated toward the end of the session you might be tempted to just end it and send people home. Would you want to be the family member waiting at home when that angry/upset person arrives? Probably not. Don't send your group out in that mood. Calm things down before they leave. If appropriate to the group, end with a prayer.

Q: Why does it work?

A: Time outs are typically effective, but many people have trouble just sitting still. Having a focus gives people who are fidgety something to do. Candles are also soothing and can transcend religious differences. If you're in a Christian group, you can make lighting the candle a ritual at the beginning, reminding everyone that the light of Christ is in your midst. In a mixed-faith or secular group, you can still do a ritual lighting and just say something like "We are a light for others." Don't take a lot of time, but calling attention to a simple and brief ritual at the beginning is better than making that kind of statement at the moment you need it. The latter can sound like scolding and defeat the purpose. If you establish the purpose at the beginning, you can just let the soothing flame do its work when you need it

Group Covenant

Q: What is it?

A: A document outlining group expectations that everyone reviews and agrees to at the first session.

Q: When do you need it?

A: Always, for every group you lead, both in person and online. It's great if you can have it posted.

Q: What do you say?

A: "It's always helpful if groups have some sort of guidelines for how to function, how we deal with our differences, and what is expected of group members. I have some basic things written here that I want to go over; we can add or adapt them for our group. Some of these things may seem overly basic, but it never hurts to go over them again."

Q: What do you do?

A: The process is laid out for you in the first session of each study. You can find the process in session one on p. 23 and the recommended covenant at the back of this Leader's Guide on p. 91. That same covenant also appears in the back of each of the student books. If have experience with a different model and find that more helpful, that's fine. What's important is to have a general covenant or code of conduct, let your specific group review it, make additions or changes, and then formally agree to keep it.

Q: Why does it work?

A: Having an objective standard for behavior and expectations allows you to refer back to the document when things go awry without it sounding like an attack on a particular person. Along the way, someone in your group may go off the rails and become "difficult." In that moment, it is easier to say, "Let's remember our group covenant," than it is to look like you're making up rules on the spot to counter one person's behavior. If you find you need to recall the covenant more than once—or if you know there are people in the group who could use the reminder—it might be helpful to simply have it posted at all group sessions.

LEADER, KNOW THYSELF

We have the most control over ourselves. Doing some gentle self-examination will help both you and your group navigate awkward moments or other issues in the dynamics of your group. The following points will help you think through some issues before they arise, making it more likely that you will deal with any problems appropriately.

1. There are no "difficult people." There are behaviors that are difficult to deal with. Try to keep judgments about behavior separate from the people who are acting out.

2. Ask yourself: Is the group having an issue with one member's behavior or did a person just hit a pet peeve or insecurity of mine? Watch body language in other group members. Do they look uncomfortable? What happens with the discussion? Does it become more lively? More heated? Does it shut down? Those observations can help you discern whether it is a group issue or your own personal issue. If you seem to be the only one bothered and the group is constructively engaged, take a deep breath and let it go.

3. Everyone is capable of being "difficult" under the right circumstances, including you.

4. Know your own strengths and weaknesses and what brings out both the best and the worst in you. Then make sure when group sessions roll around, you have set yourself up to be at your best.

5. If you are going through a difficult time in your life, you should think twice about leading a group. If the group ends up shifting to meet your own needs rather than the needs of the group members, you are likely to exhibit difficult behaviors and have a less successful group. With other serious issues on

your mind, you will also have less energy to devote to each session and may respond less effectively when group issues arise.

6. Sometimes people have legitimate criticisms about your leadership. Try to listen without becoming defensive, even if they don't communicate their issues tactfully. Is what they are saying true? Don't berate yourself. Admit any mistakes (with humor if you can) and work on improvement. That gives the group a great role model for doing the same.

7. Life happens. A quote often attributed to Plato reads, "Be kind, for everyone is fighting a great battle." Whether you are facing a cranky friend after a hard day or a demon spawn ruining your life yet again, everyone is trying to get through this life with as little damage as possible. Be kind, even when you have to be firm. Don't add to the damage.

8. As a leader, you have to deal with issues affecting your group. Being kind doesn't mean putting your head in the sand. If issues are not resolved, soon the only ones left in your group will be you and the person being difficult. If you don't feel capable of handling it, find someone else outside the group who can step in on your behalf.

9. If your group is composed of people with diverse ethnic or cultural backgrounds, do some research. What is "difficult" in some cultures is considered polite or expected in others.

TIPS FOR AVOIDING SMALL GROUP HEADACHES

Most of the problems groups encounter could have been prevented with a little effort back when the group was just a gleam in someone's eye. Plan ahead and you will have taken a dozen possible issues off the table.

1. **Be clear about the nature and purpose of the group.** Why are you starting this group? What is the need? Who can come? When and where will you meet? Will new people be welcome once the group is underway? How long will each session last? Is a financial commitment needed? Is a certain level of expertise expected? How many group sessions will there be? Will there be child care? Is the meeting space handicap accessible? There are a whole host of questions that people will want answers to before deciding whether your group is for them or not. Figure all that out before you advertise the group.

2. **Once you've advertised the group and its details, don't change it.** People signing up for this series don't want to discover it's become a prayer and support group halfway through. People thinking they can come whenever it is convenient, with no additional commitments, may discover that there's homework and they can't miss a session. Tell people exactly what to expect up front. Then give them what they signed up for.

3. **Make sure you are in a good, comfortable space.** (See below for more on this.) Uncomfortable people are cranky people. Cranky people are less able to keep any annoying personality traits in check—and more likely to present problems during group sessions.

4. **Be prepared for each and every session.** If you are figuring out what to do on the fly, people will notice. If you don't care about how the session goes, why should they? If the group has homework, you must do it also. Come on time, have everything ready, make sure cleanup is handled and any other post-session work is done.

5. **Know and use the tools at your disposal.** Know the tools that are helpful before you need them. That will help you smoothly navigate troubled waters with far less stress.

6. **Respectfully, privately, but firmly deal with issues that arise.** If a problem is allowed to fester and it becomes clear to the group that you are avoiding dealing with it, your group will suffer. Knowing someone in charge will deal with the issues lowers anxiety in all group members and lessens the chance of a group meltdown. If you do not feel equipped to deal with an issue directly, calling in help from another qualified person outside the group still counts as you dealing with it.

7. **Model the behavior outlined in your group covenant.** All of us can be difficult at times. Know your own flaws and watch them. Don't let the problem person in your group be you!

ELEMENTS OF A GOOD LEARNING SPACE FOR SMALL GROUPS

As mentioned in item #3, uncomfortable people are cranky people, and cranky people can make for difficult discussions in small groups. While you can't control whether someone is in pain or what has happened in their lives prior to arriving at your group, you can control what they encounter when they arrive. Your goal is to have people walk through the door into your session and think to themselves, "Ahhhhh...now I can put everything else aside. I'm so glad I'm here." The following are all things to consider when selecting your meeting space and preparing for the group's arrival.

1. **Good lighting.** For this study that means bright enough to read by yet not causing glare. If you can avoid fluorescent lighting, please do. There is a slight flicker to fluorescent lighting that can trigger headaches and other issues in some people.

2. **Comfortable room temperature.** A 2006 study showed that 72 degrees Fahrenheit is optimal for both learning and mood.[1] High levels of humidity lower concentration. Listen to your group members and watch the body language. Plan for a well-ventilated space where you can control the temperature and adjust as needed.

3. **Good sight lines.** Small groups in the way we're using the term are not lectures to a small number of people. They include discussion with both the group leader and other members. The space should allow for everyone to see the group leader and anything that might be posted for the group as well as one another.

4. **Allow for movement.** As group members shift to talk with different people, adjust for hearing or visual impairments, or leave to use the restroom, they shouldn't have to climb over others to do it. If you have people packed in like sardines, you need a bigger space. Seating should not be bolted down (looking at you, church pews). Judge the needs of your group for accessibility concerns. Anyone have trouble with stairs? Do floors or walkways have edges that make tripping easy? Is your space excluding the church member in a wheelchair?

5. **Distraction free.** Some of the best small groups meet in homes. But if the home is buzzing with the activities of children, pets, or other family members, go somewhere else. Look at what is on the walls and evaluate whether those items might be distracting or otherwise difficult for any in the group. Do you want your group to be interfaith or inclusive of secular folks? Maybe a room filled with Jesus and crosses isn't optimal.

6. **Comfortable seating.** Small groups typically meet for longer than an hour. Do you want to spend two hours sitting on a medieval torture device? No one else does either. Evaluate the needs of those in your group. Those with back problems may need firm seating. Others may need chairs with arms to help them get up and down.

7. **Refreshment.** Have you ever rushed to a meeting after missing a meal? Chances are pretty good that someone in your group has arrived hungry or thirsty. At the very least have a pitcher of water available. There's no need to lay out a seven-course meal for meetings, but water and a bunch of grapes can help revive the weary and keep them engaged.

8. **Appropriate surface space for activities.** So your group members now have a glass of water and some grapes and the book you're using for discussion. "Turn to page 83," you say, and the juggling begins. The water goes at their feet on the floor, where the person next to them accidentally kicks it over. Grapes are on the lap as they turn to the page in their book. Now there's something they would like to make a note about. Grapes roll. You see the issue. Most small groups are comfortable around a table or tables, or at least tray tables or end tables or something within easy reach of each participant.

---

1 Olli Seppänen, William J Fisk, and QH Lei, *Effect of Temperature on Task Performance in Office Environment* (Berkely, CA: Ernest Orlando Lawrence Berkeley National Laboratory, July 2006). https://indoor.lbl.gov/sites/all/files/lbnl-60946.pdf.

PRIORITIES

The Path to Justice

PREPARING TO LEAD SESSION ONE

At least a week before the session:

- Ask participants to bring a Bible if they have one.
- Secure enough student books for your group or make sure participants have enough time to order the books themselves.
- If group members have the books in time, it's helpful but not necessary to have them read the Introduction and chapter one before the first session. Doing so will cut down on the reading they have to do before week 2.
- Secure comfortable meeting space with tables and good lighting. (See the section in the Introduction called Elements of a Good Learning Space for Small Groups on p. 17.)
- Plan for refreshments.
- Read through the introductory material in this guide.
- Pay special attention to the introductory section called "In One Voice" on p. 12. Select the song(s) you will use throughout the study. You may choose from the list on p. 89 in this guide or from your own resources. Pick a second choice, just in case the group has a problem with your first choice.
- Think about the personalities of those who have signed up for the study. Consider whether using a talking stick as described in the Introduction to this guide (p. 14) would help ensure that everyone has an opportunity to speak during discussions.

Objectives

- To begin to learn about one another and what each of us finds important.
- To establish a covenant for the group's future discussions.
- To examine our own highest priorities and values and compare them to those given by God in the Bible.
- To think about the nature and scope of justice.
- To imagine, in concrete terms, what justice looks like when a society has achieved it in order to better judge whether we are headed in the right direction.

Materials Needed

- Newsprint or whiteboard and appropriate markers
- Paper and pens for participants
- Bibles for those who don't bring one (any translation is fine and they can be a mix)
- Student books if they don't already have them
- Nametags
- Simple refreshments, if appropriate to the setting, are always a nice touch at every session, but especially the first and last.
- Lyrics, song sheets, or other tools needed to teach the opening/closing song(s) for "In One Voice."
- Small sheets of paper for the bingo game
- An object for a talking stick (more for multiple groups if you decide to divide the larger group for some exercises)
- An easy means of keeping time
- Perhaps a cell phone or other camera to save your work from the Imagining Justice exercise. You may also simply choose to save it to paper or a laptop.

Handouts

- Social Justice Bingo (p. 81)
- Imagining Justice (p. 83)
- Beyond the Bend (p. 85)

Preparation

- Find and prepare needed materials and handouts as listed on page 19.
- Copy the handouts either from the back of this guide or download and copy from the website (massbible.org/priorities-handouts). Provide one of each for each member of the group.
- Read the Introduction and chapter one of the student book.
- Study the session instructions in this guide to understand the flow and purpose of each item. Be familiar enough with them that you can answer questions from the group if they have them.
- Read through both the handouts with their instructions, as well as the instructions in this leader's guide.
- Think about whether you will divide your group in the exercises where that is suggested and, if so, where the smaller groups will go within the space. Here are some points to consider in that decision:
    - How large is your group? If you have more than eight or ten people, consider dividing the group into two or three smaller groups at the point noted in the handout (Part I, item 3).
    - It's common for groups who know one another to want to stick together, but this often results in quieter members never having an opportunity to speak.
    - Smaller groups also allow talkers to speak more in depth, while still giving everyone a chance.
    - By nature, the more introverted folks will likely never complain about a large group discussion, but it's your job as the leader to make sure everyone who wants to say something has that opportunity.
    - Some are intimidated by speaking in front of a larger group—even when they know the people.
    - Others simply need a bit more time to reflect before they speak, and large groups can move on without them, depriving the group of sharing their thoughtful opinions.
    - Be familiar with the entire exercise ahead of time and seriously consider dividing the group for the marked sections if your group is large.
- Look up all the Bible passages you will be using in the session. Mark them so you can find them easily.

ICEBREAKER

SOCIAL JUSTICE BINGO (10 MIN.)

Objective: To begin learning about one another, to consider the breadth of social issues, and to begin sharing a bit of what is important for each person.

PART I (5 MIN.)

- Make sure each person has a small sheet of paper. Ask each person to write the three social issues they feel most passionate about, then turn the page over so others can't see it. *Note: If you have fewer than ten people, have each person write four or five social issues.*

- Give out the handout called "Social Justice Bingo" on p. 81 of this guide.

- Instruct participants to fill out the empty boxes on the bingo card with social issues. They may draw from the list on the handout or include their own. They don't have to be the ones they picked as important for them. Any issues debated in the public square are fine. When all have filled in their empty boxes, move to Part II.

PART II (5 MIN.)

- Going around the room, ask each person to give their name (assuming there are some in the group who don't know each other) and ask them to read just one of the three issues on their personal list. Note: They should only read the issue, not say what position they take or anything about why it's important.

- As issues are read, have everyone look for that issue on their bingo card and mark the card if it appears. The first person to get a bingo wins.[2] If no one wins after each person has shared one of their issues, do a second round with the second issue on their list, and so on until either someone gets bingo or the lists are exhausted.

- If no one has won by the time everyone has shared their items, you as the leader should read random issues from the list provided on the handout until someone wins.

---

[2] For those unfamiliar with the game, a "bingo" is when a card has marks across all items in a vertical, horizontal, or diagonal row.

IN ONE VOICE

(5 MIN.)

- Explain that every week you will begin with the same short song. Announce the opening song you have chosen, and reassure the group that their singing ability isn't important.

- Ask the group if the song brings up unpleasant emotions or memories for anyone. If there's even a single person for whom this is true, pick another song.

- Teach the song. You might provide it on a handout, play a recording, call on a musician, or use another method, but don't assume that everyone remembers the words or knows the tune. Sing it through a couple of times.

- Often someone initiates joining hands or some other form of physical contact during a song, which can be problematic for some. If you see this begin, quickly indicate that anyone who does not want physical contact can put their hands together in a prayer posture during the song.

My Notes

GROUP COVENANT

(10 MIN.)

Objective: To establish ground rules for discussions, which will help avert disruptive conflict.

- Ask everyone to turn to the group covenant on p. 207 at the end of the student book.
- Have volunteers read the six principles aloud, with a different person reading each one.
- Ask whether everyone is comfortable with this covenant and willing to commit to it.
- Ask if there is anything anyone would like to add.

If not already mentioned by the group, raise the question of the use of technology and social media during and after group sessions. For example:

- How will your group deal with cell phones?
- Are you open to having someone using Twitter to describe the class sessions to their followers?
- What about posting comments about class on social networking sites like Facebook?
- Write any suggestions on the newsprint/whiteboard and ask if students are willing to make these a part of their covenant. If there are items the group agrees to add, ask each student to add them on the blank lines on the group covenant page in their individual student book.

EXERCISE

IMAGINING JUSTICE HANDOUT (50 MIN.)

Objective: To help group members think through the meaning of justice by identifying the fundamentals of God's priorities as described in Scripture, defining their own most important values, and composing their own image/description of what a world with those priorities in place would be like.

BEFORE YOU BEGIN

1. Have your materials ready to record the brainstorming the group will do in Part I. Make sure the group has writing materials.

2. Give everyone a copy of the Imagining Justice handout (at the back of this guide on p. 83 and make sure they all have Bibles (translation does not matter) and their student books. It's okay if they haven't had a chance to read anything in their student books yet.

3. As you proceed, keep an eye on the clock. The themes of these discussions can easily take up all the time and more. Keep the objective of this exercise in mind (it's listed at the top) and make sure you're moving the group along, even if more could be said in response to a question.

4. If you do not divide the group, you will not need the third part of this exercise and can add five minutes more to both Part I and Part II.

PART I (20–25 MIN.)

1. Read them the objective for the exercise as listed at the beginning of this exercise. (This is not on the handout.)

2. Ask a volunteer to read the first paragraph on the handout aloud. (Note: This could be you, it could be one person, or you could have different people take turns reading. Just don't force anyone to read who may not want to.)

3. Explain that this series starts from the three examples of God's priorities listed on the handout. Ask for different volunteers to read each of the items listed. For the Ten Commandments, have the volunteer read the short-form list in the Introduction in the student book on p. 11 instead of the longer biblical passages.

4. If you do not divide the group, you will continue to serve as the leader and lead the discussion in the rest of Part I (listed on the handout), for the

next 25 minutes. If you will divide the group, see the instructions in the box below and the divided groups will have only 20 minutes.

5. When you get to questions 3 and 4 in Part I, ask for a volunteer to record responses where all can see them. Stop this discussion at the end of the first 25 minutes and move to Part II.

Dividing the Group

If you will be dividing the group, do so after the Bible passages with God's priorities have been read in Part I on the handout. Explain that the smaller groups will give more people a chance to speak at length and that the group will come back together at the end.

There may be a natural division or you can have everyone count off or use some other way to divide them. Don't spend too much time on this. The objective is just to have smaller groups so everyone can speak—and speak for a longer time.

It's helpful if the groups have some physical separation, but they don't need to go to separate rooms unless your main space is very small. Having them in the same room will help you ensure they are keeping to the time frame and to know when both groups are finished.

It's ideal for each smaller group to have a whiteboard or newsprint for brainstorming, if possible. If not, just be sure that everyone has paper for notes. Each group should also have at least one Bible—any translation is fine.

Give these instructions to the divided groups before they begin discussion:

1. Each group should pick a leader to guide the discussion and a separate person to record responses for the group to report back at the end.

2. Explain that all the instructions and discussion questions for the sections to come are on the handout. They can read it verbatim if they want, just leaving time for discussion of the questions. Let them know that you will keep track of the time and, when the 20 minutes allotted for Part I are up, you will urge them to move to Part II.

3. Remind everyone that they don't have to fully discuss every question to complete the section. The questions are there in case discussion gets stuck and to help people think about different angles. As long as the group is talking about the topic generally and is coming up with a description, they're fine.

4. Remind leaders to make space for everyone who wants to speak. If you have decided to use talking sticks, give them to the smaller group leaders now and explain how they work.

5. Lastly, tell participants that they should come back to the larger group at the end of Part II being able to describe their vision of a world in which the priorities established in Part I are lived out by all. The group reporter should be prepared to describe this to the larger group. This description should be as specific as possible (there are helps in the Part II instructions), but they don't need to produce something that will win the Nobel prize for literature. They shouldn't sweat in crafting the final product.

PART II VISIONS OF JUSTICE (20–25 MIN.)

1. If the group is divided, your job is to keep them all on track and be available if they run into snags or have questions. A divided group will have 20 minutes for this section.

2. If you maintain one group, you will lead them through the steps and questions in Part II as described on the handout. A single group will have 25 minutes for this section, and you can ignore Part III.

3. Record the group's vision in a way that can be retrieved for reference in later sessions of the study.

4. If the group is divided, call time at the end of 20 minutes and bring the groups back together and move to Part III.

PART III (10 MIN.)

1. If the group has been divided, work with a scribe at the board or newsprint to combine the visions from the various groups into one description for the group as a whole.

2. In either case, the final outcome should be a written description of the group's ideal society of justice and peace that is clear enough to go back to in later sessions of this study. Use whatever language for this that helps people think. It might be "heaven," "beloved community," "Kingdom of God," "perfect world," "utopian society"—whatever resonates with your tradition and group. Make it as detailed as you have time for.

3. If you have someone who can later turn that written description into a visual image, either through a hand drawing or computer graphics, that is a nice bonus for your group to have. You will revisit your group's ideal later in this study, so you need to save it in some form. You or someone in the group can take a picture of it, save it on paper, or whatever works best in your setting. Someone outside the group could also create an actual image using the group's written description.

Helps for Creating Your Justice Vision

- Think about all of your senses:
  - What does it look like? Is it a city, a pastoral scene, a village? Is there water? Who and what do you see? Are there animals? Birds? Bugs? Fish? Trees? Flowers?
  - What does it smell like?
  - What can you touch? What does it feel like?
  - What do you eat? What are the tastes?
  - What sounds do you hear?
- Think about how you would describe this life to people in a variety of circumstances:
  - How would you describe it to a disabled or sick child?
  - How would you describe it to an abused or neglected child?
  - How would you describe it to an elderly person who lived alone?
  - How would you describe it to someone who hates their job or has no job?
  - How would you describe it to a homeless person or someone barely scraping by?
  - How would you describe it to a frightened or anxious person?
  - How would you describe it to someone who has been persecuted or discriminated against?

My Notes

READING

BEYOND THE BEND HANDOUT (5 MIN.)

Objective: To help clarify the scope of working for justice.

- Give everyone a copy of the handout, "Beyond the Bend."
- Going around the room, ask people to take turns reading a paragraph. Make it clear that those who don't want to read can just say "pass."
- Explain that part of the purpose of this series is to help us recognize when we are just tending to the bodies without trying to fix the source of the problem and that justice is only achieved when we do both.
- Let them know that this story is discussed more in the chapter one reading.

REVIEWING HOMEWORK

(5 MIN.)

Objective: To make sure everyone understands what they should do before the next session.

Give the following instructions for preparing for the next session:

- Read the Introduction and chapters one and two in the student book. If they've already read the Introduction and chapter one before this session, they don't need to reread it.

- Pay particular attention to the final section in chapter two, "On the March: Preparing for Your Second Group Session," and reflect on the questions at the end of that section.

- Explain that a similar section will appear at the end of each chapter to help them prepare for one of the exercises in the group. Even if they don't have time to read the entire chapter, they should do their best to read this part so they can be ready for the group.

- Write out a one-sentence answer to the Check-in questions at the end of chapter two. There is space in the student book to write these.

- Explain that they will have the same Check-in questions at the end of each chapter and will be asked to share their one-sentence answer at the start of each session but won't be asked to elaborate. Let them know that the objective is to remind people of what they have read and to refocus them at the start of each group meeting.

- Lastly, assure everyone that while they will get far more from the group if they do the homework, they should not feel that they can't come to the next session if something comes up and they haven't done it. Exercises are designed in a way that even those who haven't done the homework can participate.

My Notes

IN ONE VOICE

(5 MIN.)

- Follow the instructions for the opening song for your closing. If you are using the same song, you can just repeat it. Otherwise you will need to teach it and check to be sure it poses no problems for anyone in the group.

My Notes

PRETENDERS

How to Spot an Idol

PREPARING TO LEAD SESSION TWO

Objectives

- To make sure the group understands that the term "idol" defines the way something functions rather than what the thing is.
- To think about that definition through concrete examples from daily life.
- To analyze the various stages of a conflict and how to notice when those stages are not progressing as they should.
- To consider the ways that something functioning as an idol can block the natural resolution of an issue—and that to block the resolution of an issue is to block justice.
- To examine the many forms that protest can take and to share experiences with protest of any kind.
- To recognize that protest is a predictable symptom and helpful signal that the natural resolution of an issue is blocked.
- By focusing on protest, you are helping the group to prepare to read and discuss the very specific protest of taking a knee during the national anthem, which will be discussed in session three.

Materials Needed

- Newsprint or whiteboard and appropriate markers
- Paper and pens for notes
- Talking stick
- Student book
- Nametags
- Simple refreshments
- An easy means of keeping time
- Song sheets or any other items needed for the "In One Voice" segments

Preparation

- Find and prepare needed materials as listed for this lesson.
- Read chapter two of the student book and do the preparation in the student book.
- Study the session instructions in this guide to understand the flow and purpose of each item. Be familiar enough with them that you can answer any questions from the group.
- Revisit the concept of the talking stick on p. 14 so that you are prepared to use it.

IN ONE VOICE

(5 MIN.)

- Gather your group with your opening song.

CHECK-IN

(10 MIN.)

Objective: To focus the group on the topic and remind participants of what they have read.

- What is one thing that was new to me in this material?

- What is one question that this week's topic raises for me?

DISCUSSION

(30 MIN.)

Objective: To allow people time to discuss the reading they did for homework and to get clarification on things that puzzled them or to further explore things that interest them in the material.

You have a half hour for discussion of the reading. Don't get into discussions about protests here, since that is the subject of the next exercise. You can either explore responses to the Check-in questions, ask your own questions, or use the following questions to spur discussion. If a particular question doesn't get things going, just move on. You don't have to explore every question—these queries are just helps to get people talking about the reading:

- What does having no other gods mean to you?

- Did your understanding of idols change as a result of reading this chapter?

- Have you ever discovered that you were more attached to a particular object, person, or idea than you should be? How did you finally realize it?

- You read about the issue of cigarette smoking in U.S. life and politics. Have you ever watched the whole lifespan of an issue play out, from birth to resolution, either at home, at work, or in local, state, or national politics?

- If so, what was the issue? Was it allowed to go through a natural process of people working it out or did something cause it to stall or become more divisive than it should have been?

- Has there been a time when you've helped resolve a difficult conflict? Have you seen others do so? What helped bring the problem to resolution? What made resolution more difficult?

- Does the description of idolatry as it's been presented so far make sense to you? Do you have anything to add?

- Have you ever seen an idol at work in your church, home, or workplace? What was it?

- The text mentions money as a common idol that often makes solving issues more difficult. What other kinds of idols are there? What are other powerful forces that also commonly make trouble for us? *(Note: If people are having trouble, you could suggest things like the power of celebrity, sex, prestige, military power, pride, large corporate interests, partisanship—both secular and religious—and so on. You may want to write these on your whiteboard or newsprint.)*

My Notes

EXERCISE

ON THE MARCH (45 MIN.)

Objective: To help people gain a more nuanced understanding of protest, to appreciate the human struggles behind those who disrupt the normal flow of business in these ways, and to better evaluate our actions by hearing how protest can affect the lives of others. This is also preparation for dealing with the specific issue of the NFL protest in chapter three.

Using the talking stick, you will ask people to share their experiences with protests of any kind in response to the questions they were asked to think about in the homework.

1. Tell the group that they will have a chance to share experiences they have had with various kinds of protests and that you have a list of ground rules for that sharing. Then go through the following:
   - Participants will use a talking stick. Only the person with the stick (or whatever the object is) may speak.
   - When a person is finished or when time is up, you will direct who gets the stick next.
   - While sharing, each person should focus on his or her own feelings and experiences.
   - People should not respond to the person who spoke before them, but simply tell their own story and share the way it affected them.
   - Let participants know that as you announce each question, you'll give 30 seconds for people to think about it before giving the stick to whoever wants to speak.
   - No one is required to share.
   - Encourage people to be brief so that more have an opportunity to share. Make it known that you will bring a person's sharing to a close at the end of five minutes if they haven't wrapped up already.

2. With those rules established, go through the questions below one at a time. Read a question to the group and then pause for about 30 seconds to let people think about whether they want to respond to that question. Then ask for a show of hands and pass the stick until everyone who wants to speak has had a chance to do so.

If you have a large group and a lot of people speak, you may not get to many of the questions. If you finish a question and have only a few minutes left, jump to the closing question.

- Have you ever participated in a protest of any sort? A march, a boycott, a strike, a sit-in, blocking access to something, refusing to do something your job required, or some other disruptive action guided by principle? If so, what was that experience like? What moved you to take that action? What did you want? Do you think your efforts were effective?

- Have you ever had your life disrupted by the protest of others? Did you understand what was being protested? Did it make you angry? Sympathetic? How did you respond?

- Have you or a company or organization you are a part of ever been the object of any kind of protest? What was the response? Did the issue get resolved?

- Have you ever agreed with a cause but objected to the form of a protest? What was your objection? What do you think would be more effective if the normal channels to resolving the issues are blocked?

- Have you ever either witnessed or been part of a protest that turned violent? How did you respond? How can authorities help ensure that protests remain peaceful?

3. The final question will take the form of a prayer. Make sure people can easily pass the stick from one to the next. Then invite them to complete this sentence as a closing prayer for the exercise. When they have completed the sentence they should pass the stick to the person next to them. Those who don't wish to speak should take the stick, say "pass," and give it to the person next to them.

- Finish this sentence: "It is my hope and prayer that all who protest …"

- When all are finished, you may close with "Amen" or something similar.

REVIEWING HOMEWORK

(5 MIN.)

Objective: To make sure everyone understands what they should do before the next session.

- Read chapter three.
- Do the Check-In questions at the end of the chapter and pay special attention to the reading and questions in the final section called "Taking a Knee: Preparing for Your Third Group Session."

IN ONE VOICE

(5 MIN.)

- Dismiss your group with your closing song.

ALGIANCE

How Idols Confuse Our Priorities

PREPARING TO LEAD SESSION THREE

Objectives

- To allow group members to share their experiences with the flag, anthem, and other national symbols. To consider how those experiences shape our responses to others.

- To consider how other nations honor their symbols and how we respond to the symbols of other nations.

- To talk generally about the history of our national symbols presented in the reading and to identify places where something might be functioning as an idol.

- To consider the issue of the NFL protest in depth, understand how the issue began and unfolded, and be able to share with one another points of agreement or disagreement.

- To analyze the array of power dynamics at work in the NFL protest and to consider which, if any, of those might have functioned as an idol.

- To distinguish between things that upset us because of our own background and experiences and things that violate the values and priorities of our faith.

Materials Needed

- Newsprint or whiteboard and appropriate markers
- Paper and pens for notes
- Talking stick
- Student book
- Nametags
- Simple refreshments
- An easy means of keeping time
- Song sheets or any other items needed for the "In One Voice" segments

Preparation

- Find and prepare needed materials as listed for this lesson.

- Read chapter three of the student book and do the work in the student book to prepare for the "Take a Knee" exercise. Prepare your own answers to the three questions posed in the exercise, just in case the group can't easily come up with those responses.

- Study the session instructions in this guide to understand the flow and purpose of each item. Be familiar enough with the instructions that you can answer any questions from the group.

- Decide if you're going to divide the group for the "Take a Knee" exercise.

- Revisit the concept of the talking stick on p. 14 so that you are prepared to use it.

IN ONE VOICE

(5 MIN.)

- Gather your group with your opening song.

CHECK-IN

(10 MIN.)

Objective: To focus the group on the topic and remind participants of what they have read.

- What is one thing that was new to me in this material?

- What is one question that this week's topic raises for me?

DISCUSSION

(30 MIN.)

Objective: To allow people time to discuss the reading they did for homework, to clarify things that puzzled them, and to further explore things that interested them.

You have a half hour for discussion of the reading. Don't get into questions about Kaepernick and taking a knee, since that is the subject of the exercise to come. You can either explore responses to the Check-in questions, ask your own questions, or use the following questions to spur discussion:

- Invite people who might have been raised in a different country to share the pledge, salute, anthem, or traditions that they have experienced.

- It's a stretch, but if you have very senior group members, ask if anyone remembers the old Bellamy salute.

- Have you been to a place or event where the flag of another country was honored? What did you do at that time? If not, what do you think is appropriate for someone to do when the flag of another country is presented—at the Olympics, for example?

- Ask just for a show of hands for how many people have served in the military, have a flag displayed in their home, or belong to various patriotic civil groups. Allow people to share what it means to them.

- Thinking of whatever patriotic songs you know, if you were on the committee to choose a national anthem for the United States, what would you pick, and why?

- The Flag Code states that the flag should never be used as wearing apparel, bedding, or drapery—yet people do this all the time. What are your thoughts about this practice?

- Is there more you'd like to know about these topics? What are your questions?

SESSION THREE: ALLEGIANCE

EXERCISE

TAKE A KNEE (45 MIN.)

Objective: To examine the specific issue of the NFL protests begun by Colin Kaepernick and use it to identify the way powerful people, ideas, organizations, and symbols can become idols that cause division and block the resolution of a problem.

Start by reviewing the three fact-based questions participants were asked to record at the end of their reading. Explain that this is just to make sure everyone is on the same page before moving to the more substantive discussion. The answers were all in their reading.

1. What was Colin Kaepernick's reason for protesting?
2. Why did he change the form of his protest from sitting to kneeling?
3. How did the league respond?

Check to be sure everyone had basically the same answers. If not, come to a consensus, then move on.

If you didn't do it before the session began, write out the following on the newsprint or whiteboard:

POWERFUL INFLUENCES ON THE ISSUE

- The flag and national anthem
- The multi-billion-dollar NFL industry
- An iconic brand (Nike)
- The president of the U.S.
- Social media
- Broadcast media
- Celebrity players
- Racial bias
- Attitudes toward law enforcement

Next, lead a discussion of the following questions either as one group or divided into smaller groups if you have a lot of people. Get to as many questions as you can. If time is running short and you still have a number of questions to go, skip down and make sure you do question 8 before time is up.

My Notes

If people are consistently talking over each other or if the conversation is being dominated by one or two people, consider using the talking stick or dividing into smaller groups.

1. There were lots of powerful forces at work over the life of this issue. Consider the list of those forces we've written out. Are there even more you can think of? Did any one of them have a bigger influence than the others? Did that influence make things better or worse?

2. What do you think should have been the primary concern for those trying to resolve the standoff? Did that issue remain central during the debate or was it shifted to something else? If it was shifted, how did that change affect the debate?

3. Which parties were directly involved and naturally belonged at the table to resolve the issue? Did any of them get overshadowed by less central interests or powers? If so, how did that change help or hinder the problem?

4. Remember the five signs of an idol's presence:
   - Bad fruit
   - A powerful thing has inserted itself where it doesn't belong
   - Proposed solutions are all win-lose instead of win-win
   - There are lies and deception about the real issue
   - It's an all-or-nothing choice

   Do you think any idols were at work during the most divisive time of this issue?

5. Protests of all kinds are supposed to raise awareness about a problem and push those who can do something to help fix it. Do you think the NFL protests accomplished their goal of raising awareness and demanding action about racial injustice?

6. Outside of formal games, Colin Kaepernick wore some clothing that angered people, notably wearing socks of pigs in police hats and a shirt that showed Fidel Castro and Malcolm X in dialogue. What effect do you think such personal choices have on the larger cause for which a person is advocating? How can we distinguish between the message and the messenger in such circumstances?

7. Celebrities in all fields have a large public platform, allowing them to raise awareness on a large scale very quickly. Do you think they should use that platform to champion a cause? Are there some causes they should stay away from? For example, should they only advocate for causes within their particular industry or should they be able to take up whatever concerns them?

8. As you look back on the controversy, what part(s) of it do you think Jesus would be concerned about? Are there pieces of it that match any of God's priorities? What kind of actions can help get us back on the path to justice in this situation?

REVIEWING HOMEWORK

(5 MIN.)

Objective: To make sure everyone understands what they should do before the next session.

- Remind participants to read the next chapter and to do the work at the end in the section called "That's the Spirit: Preparing for Your Fourth Group Session" before your next session. Let them know that the reason they're being asked to write out their answers to the questions in that section is to help the exercise at the next session go more quickly.

IN ONE VOICE

(5 MIN.)

- Dismiss your group with your closing song.

SUPREMACY

How Idols Divide Us

PREPARING TO LEAD SESSION FOUR

Objectives

- To put our current divisions into historical context.
- To identify signs in those divisions that could indicate something is functioning as an idol.
- To think about the various "tribes" to which we belong.
- To consider and identify the artistic, cultural, and political forces that shape our understanding of who we are as a country.
- To talk generally about the history presented in the reading.
- To identify a set of characteristics that define our national spirit for your group and to compare that definition to their image of justice from session one.

Materials Needed

- Newsprint or whiteboard and appropriate markers
- Paper and pens for notes
- Talking stick
- Student book
- The description/vision of justice the group developed in session one
- Bibles (any translation or a mix of translations is fine). Since you'll only use two verses (Galatians 5:22–23), you could also just print out those verses for everyone—whichever is easier.
- Nametags
- Simple refreshments
- An easy means of keeping time
- Song sheets or any other items needed for the "In One Voice" segments

Preparation

- Find and prepare needed materials as listed for this lesson.
- Read chapter four of the student book and do the work in the student book to prepare for the "That's the Spirit" exercise.
- Look through the examples of answers to the student book questions on p. 58 of this guide. Keep that information handy to help any group that might have trouble coming up with examples.

- Study the session instructions in this guide to understand the flow and purpose of each item. Be familiar enough with them that you can answer questions from the group.

- Become familiar with the fruit of the Spirit, as described in Galatians 5:22–23.

- Think through how you will divide the group for the "That's the Spirit" exercise.

- Revisit the concept of the talking stick on p. 14 so that you are prepared to use it.

IN ONE VOICE

(5 MIN.)

- Gather your group with your opening song.

CHECK-IN

(10 MIN.)

Objective: To focus the group on the topic and remind participants of what they have read.

- What is one thing that was new to me in this material?

- What is one question that this week's topic raises for me?

DISCUSSION

(30 MIN.)

Objective: To allow people time to discuss the reading they did for homework, to clarify things that puzzled them, and to further explore things that interested them.

You have half an hour for discussion of the reading. Don't get into questions about the lists they were asked to make for homework; that is the subject of the exercise to come. You can either explore responses to the Check-in questions, ask your own questions, or use the following questions to spur discussion:

- Does your church celebrate civic holidays like the Fourth of July in Sunday morning worship? What are your thoughts about that? How could that go wrong? How could that be helpful in keeping American exceptionalism in its place?

- Were you aware of the history of "America First" before reading this chapter? Did you know about the political career of Dr. Seuss?

- What are the strengths and weaknesses of the United States and of its citizens? What do we do well? Where can we be better?

- What tribes do you see at work in your church? Your family? Your town? Are there any that cause divisions? Are there any that help bring people together?

- Do you agree with the author that nationalism is a problem? Why or why not?

- Are there other false gods that might fit with this chapter that weren't mentioned?

SESSION FOUR: SUPREMACY   53

EXERCISE

THAT'S THE SPIRIT (45 MIN.)

Objective: To help each person think deeply about how their own understanding of the U.S. was formed, to articulate an understanding of what it means to be an "American," and then to compare those understandings with both the vision of justice they developed in session one and the biblical fruit of the Spirit.

PART I (15 MIN.)

- Ask everyone to take out the responses to the questions they were asked in the final section of chapter four. (If there are some who didn't do it, they'll still be able to participate, they just won't have had the advantage of having thought about the questions ahead of time.)

- Divide into small groups of 2–3 people. (You can do this all together if you want, but smaller groups help make this part fit in the time frame.)

- Once participants are in their groups, ask them to share with one another their answers to the first four questions on p. 129 in their student books and what seemed "American" about those things. They can record them or not as they wish. They won't need to share them with the larger group. This part of the exercise is to help prepare participants to answer the later questions in Part II.

- Stop at the end of 15 minutes and bring everyone back into one group to deal with questions 5 and 6 on p. 129 in their student books for Part II.

Note: If people are stumped and need some ideas to get started in a particular category, see the lists on p. 58 of this Leader's Guide for suggestions

PART II (30 MIN.)

- Ask for a volunteer to record answers on the whiteboard/newsprint.

- Ask people to share their answers to question 5 on p. 129 in the student book, including any responses they may think of now: What are the characteristics of our national spirit as you see them? How would you describe the best of this country to someone unfamiliar with it?

- Once you have a list that includes everyone's answers, revisit the group's vision of justice that they developed in session one and have someone read it.
- Invite them to compare that ideal vision with their description of our national spirit. Are they compatible? In what way? Are there ways they don't match up?
- Next have someone read Galatians 5:22–23, which lists the fruit of the Spirit. Ask participants the same question. Are the attributes Paul lists as fruit of the Spirit compatible with those that mark the our national spirit? Are there ways they could be a better match?
- To close, ask people to read the sentence they were asked to finish in question 6 on p. 129 of the student book: "I hope that our nation…" Just go around the room and have people share without comment, as if it were a prayer.

REVIEWING HOMEWORK

(5 MIN.)

Objective: To make sure everyone understands what they should do before the next session.

- Remind the group to read the next chapter and to do the work at the end of the chapter in the section called "Monumental Decisions: Preparing for Your Fifth Group Session."

IN ONE VOICE

(5 MIN.)

- Dismiss your group with your closing song.

THAT'S THE SPIRIT HELPS

(5 MIN.)

If your group is stuck thinking of answers to the questions from their student books for this exercise, here are some responses to get them started or to add some diversity if needed.

1. Where should a tourist visit to better understand and/or appreciate the United States?

    - Yellowstone (or other national park)
    - Disney
    - Times Square
    - Ellis Island
    - Alcatraz
    - The Alamo
    - Hollywood
    - Nashville
    - The Statue of Liberty
    - Philadelphia/Liberty Bell/Independence Hall
    - Boston/Freedom Trail
    - Route 66
    - Coney Island
    - Las Vegas
    - The Smithsonian and other National Mall museums and monuments

2. What events in our history shaped us as a nation?

    - Wars (American Revolution, Civil War, WWI, WWII, Vietnam, Korea, Iraq)
    - September 11, 2001
    - The moon landing
    - Slavery/Jim Crow/Reconstruction
    - Civil Rights movement
    - Women's suffrage
    - Trail of Tears
    - Assassinations (JFK, MLK, Bobby Kennedy)
    - Mayflower
    - Any of the various waves of immigration
    - Prohibition
    - The railroad
    - The interstate highway system
    - FDR's New Deal
    - Marriage equality
    - Watergate

My Notes

3. In each of the following categories, what is at least one thing that would help a stranger get a sense of the U.S. and its people? Answers can be things from the past or present and don't have to be American in origin.

TV SHOWS

- All in the Family
- Gunsmoke
- The Honeymooners
- Little House on the Prairie
- The Mary Tyler Moore Show
- Roots
- The Brady Bunch
- Wide World of Sports
- Happy Days
- I Love Lucy
- Baseball (Ken Burns)
- The Cosby Show
- As the World Turns
- Dallas
- The Sopranos
- Saturday Night Live
- Any game show
- Any reality show

MOVIES / THEATER

- Gone With the Wind
- Star Wars
- To Kill a Mockingbird
- American Graffiti
- Mr. Smith Goes to Washington
- 12 Years a Slave
- It's a Wonderful Life
- The Godfather
- Raiders of the Lost Ark
- All the President's Men
- The Autobiography of Miss Jane Pittman
- Butch Cassidy and the Sundance Kid
- West Side Story
- Guess Who's Coming to Dinner
- Hamilton
- Oklahoma
- Rocky
- The Wizard of Oz
- Amistad

BOOKS

- Catcher in the Rye
- Uncle Tom's Cabin
- The Waste Land
- The Grapes of Wrath
- Invisible Man
- The Bible
- Huckleberry Finn
- The Handmaid's Tale
- The Great Gatsby
- Their Eyes Were Watching God
- The Scarlet Letter
- Paul Revere's Ride
- A Farewell to Arms
- Walden
- Silent Spring
- 1984
- The Bell Jar
- Beloved
- Poor Richard's Almanac
- The Last of the Mohicans
- Poetry of Edgar Allan Poe
- Moby Dick
- Leaves of Grass
- The Joy Luck Club
- On the Road

GRAPHIC ART

- American Gothic
- Peaceable Kingdom
- Christina's World
- Whistler's Mother
- Portrait of George Washington (Stuart)
- Nighthawks
- Freedom From Want (Rockwell)
- Sugar Shack
- Washington Crossing the Delaware
- Campbell's Soup Cans (Warhol)
- The Child's Bath (Cassatt)
- Ansel Adams photography
- Audubon Bird Prints
- Photograph of Sitting Bull

MUSIC

- We Shall Overcome
- American Pie
- Gospel music
- Spirituals
- Barbershop
- Rap
- Jazz
- God Bless the USA
- Take Me Home, Country Roads
- We're in the Money
- Alice's Restaurant
- Elvis
- Country
- Blues
- New World Symphony
- Rhapsody in Blue
- What a Wonderful World

5

FREEDOM

The Bulwark Against Idolatry

PREPARING TO LEAD SESSION FIVE

Objectives

- To examine the scope and implications of the First Amendment by role-playing a historical Supreme Court case.
- To reflect on the issues surrounding the erection and removal of monuments by crafting a solution to the Silent Sam dilemma in North Carolina.
- To think about solutions to a divisive issue (Confederate monuments) through the lens of faith and our core values.

Materials Needed

- Newsprint or whiteboard and appropriate markers
- Paper and pens for notes
- Student book
- Nametags
- Simple refreshments
- An easy means of keeping time
- Song sheets or any other items needed for the "In One Voice" segments

Handouts

- Cantwell v. Connecticut (p. 87)

Preparation

- Find and prepare needed materials and handouts as listed for this lesson.
- Read chapter five of the student book and do the work in the student book to prepare for the "Monumental Decisions" exercise.
- Write out the basics of the Silent Sam case as outlined in the first part of the "Monumental Decisions" exercise. Put them on the whiteboard or newsprint for easy reference.
- You will also need the Establishment and Free Exercise Clauses of the First Amendment written out for the group. You will find it at the beginning of the Church and State exercise on p. 65 in this guide.
- Read through the Cantwell v. Connecticut handout to understand what the groups should do once they have been assigned; be prepared to answer questions.

- Study the session instructions in this guide to understand the flow and purpose of each item. Be familiar enough with them that you can answer questions from the group.

- Think about how to divide the group for the two exercises.

- For the Monumental Decision exercise, write out the concerns of the university that the groups will need to consider in making a recommendation. They are listed under the second bullet point in Part I of the exercise on p. 67 of this guide.

- Research Silent Sam to see if the university has reached a decision on how to handle the remains of the statue, since that is unknown at the time of this writing. Be prepared to give any updates to the group once they have finished the exercise.

IN ONE VOICE

(5 MIN.)

- Gather your group with your opening song.

CHECK-IN

(10 MIN.)

Objective: To focus the group on the topic and remind participants of what they have read.

- What is one thing that was new to me in this material?

- What is one question that this week's topic raises for me?

EXERCISE

CHURCH AND STATE (30 MIN.)

Objective: To help group members think through the issues of free speech and the free exercise of religion by studying an actual Supreme Court case through role-play.

1. Write the following on newsprint or a whiteboard so that the whole group can see:
   - "Congress shall make no law respecting an establishment of religion, or prohibiting the free exercise thereof."
2. Explain that those words are part of the First Amendment to the U.S. Constitution and are known as the Establishment Clause and the Free Exercise Clause.
3. If the group has more than 10 people, divide the group into two, trying to place an odd number of people in each group. (Just so they don't end up with an even split and no decision.)
4. Tell participants that each group will serve as the Supreme Court of the United States, trying to uphold the Constitution. Then give them the handout called "Cantwell vs. Connecticut," explaining that this is an actual case that went before the Supreme Court in 1940, and that each group should separately debate and decide the case.
5. Refer the groups to the handout for instructions on how to proceed in their group.
6. When the groups have finished, have each chief justice share their decision and reasoning and then give them the actual results from the Supreme Court case as follows:
   - The U.S. Supreme Court overturned the Connecticut rulings, finding that Cantwell's action was protected by the First and Fourteenth Amendments. (The Fourteenth Amendment prevents states from enacting laws that abridge the constitutional rights of citizens and protects due process and equal protection for all people.)
   - Justice Owen Roberts wrote in a unanimous opinion: "Nothing we have said is intended even remotely to imply that, under the cloak of religion, persons may, with impunity, commit frauds upon the public. Certainly penal laws are available to punish such conduct. Even the exercise of religion may be at some slight

inconvenience in order that the State may protect its citizens from injury. Without doubt a State may protect its citizens from fraudulent solicitations by requiring a stranger in the community, before permitting him publicly to solicit funds for any purpose, to establish his identity and his authority to act for the cause which he purports to represent. The State is likewise free to regulate the time and manner of solicitation generally, in the interest of public safety, peace, comfort or convenience. But to condition the solicitation of aid for the perpetuation of religious views or systems upon a license, the grant of which rests in the exercise of a determination by state authority as to what is a religious cause, is to lay a forbidden burden upon the exercise of liberty protected by the Constitution."

In other words: States can stop religious groups from committing crimes or violating the Constitution. They can also protect citizens from harassment by setting some reasonable boundaries for times and places of solicitation. But a state can't regulate what is or isn't a religious cause within an already-established religious organization if the actions taken aren't otherwise against the law.

EXERCISE

A MONUMENTAL DECISION (45 MIN.)

Objective: To explore the issues surrounding divisive monuments by developing a faith-based response to a specific controversy over a Confederate monument at a university in North Carolina.

PART I (35 MIN.)

- Remind the group of the story of Silent Sam in the preparation they were asked to do for homework. Quickly cover the following basics for anyone who has forgotten or who may not have read it. Remind them that they can reference the full story beginning on p. 163 in their student books.
    - Silent Sam was erected in 1913 as a monument to those from the university who died in the Confederate army during the Civil War.
    - Funds were raised by a group who openly praised the KKK.
    - The dedication speech was given by a Civil War veteran who spoke proudly about beating a black woman very close to where the statue was placed.
    - There have been protests against the statue since the 1950s.
    - It was toppled by a large group of students in August 2018.
    - A suggestion to create a historical center on campus where the monument could be relocated resulted in a protest by the faculty and the idea was scrapped.
- Reconvene your groups, but this time, instead of being the Supreme Court, they are to assume the roles of the governing body of a church near the University of North Carolina at Chapel Hill. They know the university is wrestling with the following concerns. (Write them out where the group(s) can see them as they discuss.)
    - What to do with the remains of the monument.
    - How to represent the history of a difficult time in the life of the university.
    - How to remember those from the university who were killed or injured during the Civil War.

- How to have their public space represent the school's current values of inclusion and respect.
- How to protect students, staff, and visitors from divisive symbols, painful reminders, and potential violence.
- How to heal the divisions in the university and surrounding community that were exposed and heightened by the felling of the statue and its aftermath.

• As a church whose membership includes faculty and students from UNC, have each group offer one suggestion to the UNC trustees that could be helpful to at least one of the school's concerns in a way that would be consistent both with the church's values and the nation's commitment to the freedoms guaranteed in the First Amendment.

PART II (10 MIN.)

If you have more than one group, ask the groups to share their proposals with each other.

At the time of this writing, the university has not enacted a solution. Before conducting this exercise, do an internet search to see if a decision has been reached. If so, present the university's actual solution at the end of the exercise, as you did with the Supreme Court decision.

Ask each person to complete this sentence: "I pray that the day will come when…"

Feel free to substitute the word "hope" for "pray" if it seems a better fit for your group.

REVIEWING HOMEWORK

(5 MIN.)

Objective: To make sure everyone understands what they should do before the next session.

- Remind the group to read the next chapter and to do the work at the end of the chapter in the section called "Straight Shooter: Preparing for Your Final Group Session."

IN ONE VOICE

(5 MIN.)

- Dismiss your group with your closing song.

ARMED

How to Tame Your Idol

PREPARING TO LEAD SESSION SIX

Objectives

- To share experiences and opinions about guns.
- To be able to share those things in a supportive environment where all can be heard and thereby learn more about the issue and one another.
- To articulate those experiences in a hopeful framework that all can share.
- To evaluate the group's vision of justice from session one in light of what has been learned.
- To evaluate this study.

Materials Needed

- Newsprint or whiteboard and appropriate markers
- Paper and pens for notes
- Student book
- The description/vision of justice from session one
- Nametags
- Simple refreshments
- An easy means of keeping time
- Song sheets or any other items needed for the "In One Voice" segments

Handouts

- Final Evaluation—Participant (p. 95)

Preparation

- Find and prepare needed materials and handouts as listed for this lesson.
- Read chapter six of the student book and do the work in the student book to prepare for the exercise on guns.
- Revisit the concept of the talking stick on p. 14 so that you are prepared to use it.
- Study the session instructions in this guide to understand the flow and purpose of each item. Be familiar enough with them that you can answer questions from the group.
- When the study is finished, be sure to send in your own leader evaluation (p. 93) as well.

IN ONE VOICE

(5 MIN.)

- Gather your group with your opening song.

CHECK-IN

(10 MIN.)

Note: This is a different set of questions than those in the previous chapters.

Objective: To focus the group and to help prep everyone for being able to understand each other in the Hearing One Another exercise.

- What is one concern on the other side of the gun debate that I really can't understand?

- What is one concern on the other side of the gun debate that I really do understand?

My Notes

EXERCISE

HEARING ONE ANOTHER (60 MIN.)

Objectives: To allow people to express their views on guns in a supportive, controlled setting. To allow all views to be heard and appreciated without judgment. To encourage empathy by sharing experiences. To frame those experiences with a wish of hope.

For this, you will remain as one group. If for some reason your group is very large (more than about 18 people), you may need to divide the group so that everyone can have enough time to share. If you have a very large group and don't want to divide, you should add time to this final session.

As part of your preparation, refresh your understanding of the talking stick on p. 14 of this Leader's Guide.

- Explain that when we engage in heated debates we are often too busy trying to make our own points that we don't listen to the experiences of others. So this is an exercise to allow the group to hear one another without judging.
- Explain the following rules for the exercise:
  1. You will ask for a volunteer to share a particular kind of experience.
  2. There will be a full minute of silence for people to think and decide whether they want to share.
  3. If someone wants to share, they should raise a hand.
  4. That person will receive whatever object you are using as a talking stick. Only the person holding that object may speak.
  5. When a person is sharing, the others are to be silent and listen.
  6. Each person will have no more than five minutes. You will keep time.
  7. When a person finishes, there will be no questions or counterpoints.
  8. The person sharing may not refer back to any other speaker or the things they shared unless they are sharing about the exact same event (for example, they were both survivors of the same mass shooting).
  9. The person sharing should speak for himself or herself and no one else. You will gently remind the speaker who slips away from this rule.

10. As each person finishes sharing, he or she should add some kind of a hope for the future.
11. You will record those hopes.
12. In response to that hope, the rest of the group may respond, "Lord, hear our prayer." Those who are not religious may respond, "May it be so." (Note: The goal here is to affirm a shared hope. If there's another phrase that is a better fit for your group, use that.)
13. The final speaker gives the talking stick back to you when finished.
14. Others who want to share an experience in the same category should raise a hand and receive the stick. If not, move to the next category.
15. When you've gone through all the categories, give others a final chance to speak to any of the prior topics if they've changed their minds.
16. When all who wish have shared, recite each of the hopes again from the list you've made as a closing prayer.

- Be sure to leave a full minute (time it) for people to think before volunteering to share.
- The topic is guns and the sharing categories are:
    1. What the culture of guns was like in the home where you grew up.
    2. A time you had a positive, bonding experience with someone else that involved the use of guns.
    3. Why you don't want to own a gun.
    4. A time you lost an important relationship over differing opinions about guns.
    5. Why owning a gun is important to you.
    6. A time you or someone close to you was affected by gun violence.
    7. If you are in an area that directly experienced a mass shooting, add a category about that experience.

My Notes

SESSION SIX: ARMED

EXERCISE

IMAGINING JUSTICE (5 MIN.)

Objective: To revisit the group's vision of justice from the first session to see if anything has changed.

Invite the group to check in with their vision from session one. Now that they have completed the study, is there anything on their image they want to add, subtract, or adjust?

WRAP-UP

(15 MIN.)

Objective: To evaluate the study and collect feedback to help make the material better.

Hand out the Exploring Justice "Final Evaluation" found at the end of this guide on p. 95, along with a #10 envelope.

Ask everyone to fill it out and give it to you in the sealed envelope before leaving. Within the next week, put those evaluations into a larger envelope and mail to The Massachusetts Bible Society. The address can be found under the "Contact" tab at massbible.org. Be sure to send in your own leader evaluation (p. 93) as well.

My Notes

IN ONE VOICE

(5 MIN.)

- Dismiss your group with your closing song.

HANDOUTS

HANDOUT
SOCIAL JUSTICE BINGO

Guns				Healthcare
	Abortion		Debt	
	Sexism		Racism	
Immigration				Climate

INSTRUCTIONS
Fill in the remaining spaces by choosing additional social issues. You may pick your own or use some of the suggestions below.

Law Enforcement	LGBTQ Rights	Mass Incarceration	Wealth Inequality
Food Insecurity	Capital Punishment	Care for Veterans	Labor Laws
Marijuana Legalization	Voting Rights	Respect for Flag	Domestic Violence
Endangered Species	Ageism	Corporate Regulation	
Education	Religious Freedom	Disability Rights	
Human Trafficking	Affordable Housing	Free Speech	

HANDOUT
IMAGINING JUSTICE

PART I: PRIORITIES (20 MIN.)

Judaism recognizes 613 commandments in the Hebrew Scriptures, and in the New Testament many more laws are added for Christians. But are all commandments created equal? Most of us would be hard-pressed to believe that combining wool and linen (prohibited in Deuteronomy 22:11) is just as abhorrent to God as the murder forbidden in the sixth commandment, or that Paul's instruction that women shouldn't braid their hair (1 Timothy 2:9) is as important as the Golden Rule (Matthew 7:12). But is there some way for us to know which of the Bible's commands carry more weight? If we want to make God's priorities our priorities, where do we start? What does the Lord require of us? Is there a summary somewhere?

This series asks us to look at three summaries of God's priorities:

- The Ten Commandments: Full versions are in Exodus 20:1–17 and Deuteronomy 5:6–21. There is an abbreviated list in the student book on p. 11.
- The Great Commandment: Matthew 22:36–40
- Micah 6:6–8

Note: Large groups may divide into smaller groups at this point, coming back together after Part II. Your leader will instruct you if you should do this.

Discuss the following questions with your group:

1. What do you think of that list of passages? Do they adequately summarize God's priorities?
2. Do you think that living according to those values would lead to a healthy, just, and peaceful world? Why or why not? *Note: Discuss with the assumption that such values would be freely chosen and not imposed by law or other forms of coercion.*
3. Is anything fundamental missing from that list? Are there other passages you would add? If so, list them here:

4. Are there any other values and ideals, whether stated directly in the Bible or not, that help ensure justice and peace for society? To help get you started, think about the following:

   ○ What sort of guidelines are in place in your job or home that ensure that everyone is treated respectfully and fairly?

   ○ What values are represented by the statues of justice in our courts with their blindfolds, lamps, scales, and swords? What ideals inform them?

   ○ Don't just think of legal outcomes. What sort of behaviors would stop an injustice in the first place? What attitudes would you want children to adopt to help create a just society?

   ○ List any additional values or ideals here:

PART II: VISIONS OF JUSTICE (20 MIN.)

Note: If you have divided into smaller groups, remain there for this part.

1. The Bible has two main places where it describes a new world of justice and peace. In biblical terms, that world of justice is what the kingdom of God looks like. Volunteers should read the following two passages aloud to the group:
   - Isaiah 11:1–9
   - Revelation 21:1–8

2. Discuss the following questions:
   - Do either of those visions appeal to you? Why or why not?
   - The passage in Revelation lists certain behaviors that would result in someone being excluded from God's kingdom. Do you agree that some behaviors would be incompatible with a world of perfect justice? What do you think of the particular list in Revelation 21:8?

3. The Lord's Prayer contains the line, "Thy kingdom come, thy will be done on earth as it is in heaven." Thinking about that prayer, discuss the following:
   - Do you think it's possible for God's kingdom as described in Isaiah and Revelation to exist on earth?
   - If it did, what would it look like, specifically? If you lived there, how would you feel? How would you spend your time? How would people behave? What current problems would no longer exist and what new things might emerge? Would people live together or separately? How would conflicts be resolved? What would the natural world be like and how would people engage with it?
   - Using your lists of Bible passages, values, and ideals from the discussions so far, create a description of your group's perfect society. You can be as general or specific as you'd like, but only include things on which everyone in the group agrees. If you have divided into smaller groups for this section, assign someone to report this description back to the larger group.

Helps for Creating Your Justice Vision

- Think about all of your senses:
  - What does it look like? Is it a city, a pastoral scene, a village? Is there water? Who and what do you see? Are there animals? Birds? Bugs? Fish? Trees? Flowers?
  - What does it smell like?
  - What can you touch? What does it feel like?
  - What do you eat? What are the tastes?
  - What sounds do you hear?
- Think about how you would describe this life to people in a variety of circumstances:
  - How would you describe it to a disabled or sick child?
  - How would you describe it to an abused or neglected child?
  - How would you describe it to an elderly person who lived alone?
  - How would you describe it to someone who hates their job or has no job?
  - How would you describe it to a homeless person or someone barely scraping by?
  - How would you describe it to a frightened or anxious person?
  - How would you describe it to someone who has been persecuted or discriminated against?

HANDOUT
BEYOND THE BEND—A PARABLE

Although the origin of the story is unknown, Ronald Rolheiser tells the following story in his 1999 book The Holy Longing:[3]

> Once upon a time, there was a town that was built just beyond the bend of a large river. One day some of the children from the town were playing beside the river when they noticed three bodies floating in the water. They ran for help and the townsfolk quickly pulled the bodies out of the river.
>
> One body was dead so they buried it. One was alive, but quite ill, so they put that person into the hospital. The third turned out to be a healthy child, who then they placed with a family who cared for it and who took it to school.
>
> From that day on, every day a number of bodies came floating down the river and, every day, the good people of the town would pull them out and tend to them—taking the sick to hospitals, placing the children with families, and burying those who were dead.
>
> This went on for years; each day brought its quota of bodies, and the townsfolk not only came to expect a number of bodies each day but also worked at developing more elaborate systems for picking them out of the river and tending to them. Some of the townsfolk became quite generous in tending to these bodies and a few extraordinary ones even gave up their jobs so that they could tend to this concern full-time. And the town itself felt a certain healthy pride in its generosity.
>
> However, during all these years and despite all that generosity and effort, nobody thought to go up the river, beyond the bend that hid from their sight what was above them, and find out why, daily, those bodies came floating down the river.

---

3   Ronald Rolheiser, *The Holy Longing: The Search for a Christian Spirituality* (New York: Doubleday, 1999). Copyright © 1999 by Ronald Rolheiser. Used by permission of Doubleday, an imprint of the Knopf Doubleday Publishing Group, a division of Penguin Random House LLC. All rights reserved.

HANDOUT
CANTWELL V. CONNECTICUT

Note: This is an actual case that came before the Supreme Court in 1940.[4]

Instructions for your group:

1. Appoint a person as chief justice for the group. That person will guide deliberations, ask for the vote, and report the majority decision and reasoning when both groups are done.

2. Read all the sections in "THE CASE" aloud, with all who wish to read taking turns reading a paragraph.

3. Debate the questions on the handout (and any others you think of) and take a vote to either uphold the lower court (which convicted the Cantwells) or overturn the lower court. Majority rules.

4. When the time is up (you have 25 minutes), your chief justice will be asked to share your decision and reasoning.

THE CASE

Background

In Connecticut, state law held that the secretary of state would need to issue a permit for all solicitation. As part of that permit process, the secretary would determine whether the cause was "a religious one or is a bona fide object of charity or philanthropy" and whether the solicitation "conforms to reasonable standards of efficiency and integrity." In other words, the secretary of the State of Connecticut would issue a permit if you seemed like a legitimate religion or charity and weren't scamming people. If you passed that test, you got a permit.

What Happened

A Jehovah's Witness named Newton Cantwell, along with his two young sons, was taking his religious message door to door in New Haven, Connecticut. They did not have a permit for solicitation, but proceeded to share their faith through the heavily Catholic neighborhood, selling books and pamphlets and soliciting contributions. They also had a portable phonograph to play recordings that described the books they had for sale.

As they traveled the neighborhood, Newton's son Jesse stopped two men on the street and asked permission to play one of their records. The men agreed. The book being described on the recording was called "Enemies," which singled out the Roman Catholic Church for attack. Since the neighborhood was 90 percent Catholic, the men who heard the recording were incensed. There was no physical altercation, but they did report the Cantwells to authorities.

Newton Cantwell and his two sons were arrested and charged with violating the statute that required a permit before solicitation and inciting a common-law breach of the peace by playing an inflammatory recording to people who would likely find it offensive.

The Case in Connecticut

The Cantwells were convicted in a Connecticut court because they did not have a permit for solicitation, and because they played an inflammatory recording. They appealed, citing their right to freely exercise their religion without needing a permit from the state, as well as their right to freedom of speech. They had asked and received permission from the two men before making their presentation, and the recording had not led to violence.

The Supreme Court in Connecticut upheld their conviction, ruling that the statute requiring a permit was an effort to protect the public against fraud. Since they could receive a permit for religious purposes as long as their religion was legitimate, the higher court decided that requiring a permit did not violate the Cantwells' right to freely exercise their religion. The Connecticut Supreme Court applied the breach of the peace only to the father, but ruled that actual violence was not necessary to charge a breach of the peace.

The Cantwells questioned the state's right to determine which religions were legitimate and what constitutes inflammatory speech and appealed again to the U.S. Supreme Court.

---

[4] Information in this handout is taken from Wikipedia, s.v. "Cantwell v. Connecticut," last modified May 7, 2019, https://en.wikipedia.org/wiki/Cantwell_v._Connecticut.

Your Sworn Duty

You now sit as the Supreme Court of the United States hearing this case, making a decision that will uphold the Constitution. You must decide whether to uphold the lower court's ruling to convict the Cantwells or to overturn the ruling of the previous courts. What say you?

Below are some questions to consider as you deliberate:

1. Would this be different if had it been members of a Congregational Church challenging the Baptists, or if the Catholics had been confronting the Jehovah's Witnesses? How about if the recording demonizing the Catholics had been heard by non-Catholics?

2. Should an individual secretary of state get to decide what is a legitimate religion and what is not in order to forbid some from soliciting?

3. Did it matter that the Catholic men gave permission for the Cantwells to play their recording?

4. If you agree to hear a recording by someone soliciting on the street and it turns out to be vile and hateful toward you, is that hateful speech protected? Should it be?

5. Should everyone be free of religious solicitation?

6. Did Connecticut's conviction of the Cantwells violate their freedom to exercise their religion?

7. Did the conviction for a breach of the peace violate their right to free speech?

8. Was the secretary of state in Connecticut trying to establish only certain religions as valid in making the initial decision to deny the permit? Would that violate the Establishment Clause?

We await your decision.

RESOURCE
"IN ONE VOICE"

Look for these in a hymnal near you or online. You are also free to choose something else more to the liking of your group. These are in no particular order and may be sung in whole or in part.

SONGS FOR EITHER OPENING OR CLOSING

"On Eagle's Wings" by Michael Joncas

"Dona Nobis Pacem" (Grant Us Peace), Traditional Latin

"Bless the Lord My Soul" by Jacques Berthier (based on Psalm 103:1)

"As the Deer" by Martin J. Nystrom (based on Psalm 42:1)

"Halle, Halle, Hallelujah" by Fred Pratt Green

"Amazing Grace" by John Newton

"Give Thanks" by Henry Smith

"Simple Gifts" by Joseph Brackett

"The Servant Song" by Richard Gillard

"They'll Know We Are Christians by Our Love" by Peter Scholtes

"Make Us One" by Carol Cymbala

"Change Our Hearts" by Rory Cooney

"Joy in the Morning" by Natalie Sleeth

"Blest Be the Tie That Binds" by John Fawcett

"Help Us Accept Each Other" by Fred Kaan

"Ubi Caritas" (Live in Charity) by Jacques Berthier and the Taizé community

"You Are Mine" by David Haas

"Veni Sancte Spiritus" (Holy Spirit, Come to Us), Taizé chant, music by Jacques Berthier

"Make Me a Servant" by Kelly Willard

"More Like You" by Scott Wesley Brown

"Make Me a Channel of Your Peace," Prayer of St. Francis, adapted by Sebastian Temple

"Jesu, Jesu" Ghanaian folk song, adapted by Tom Colvin

"Be Not Afraid" by John Michael Talbot

"I Will Call Upon the Lord" by Michael O'Shields

SONGS FOR OPENING

"Gather Us In" by Marty Haugen (verse 1 or 4)

"God Is Here!" by Fred Pratt Green and Cyril V. Taylor

"Shall We Gather at the River" by Robert Lowry

"Awake, Awake, and Greet the New Morn" by Marty Haugen (especially appropriate at Advent)

"This is the Day" by Les Garrett (based on Psalm 118:24)

SONGS FOR CLOSING

"The Trees of the Field" by Steffi Geiser Ruben

"May You Run and Not Be Weary" by Paul Murakami and Handt Hanson

"Go Now in Peace" by Natalie Sleeth

"Shalom to You" by Elise S. Eslinger

"Let Us Now Depart in Thy Peace," New Mexican folk song adapted by Lee Hastings Bristol Jr.

"Shalom," Trad. Hebrew blessing

"God Be with You till We Meet Again" by Jeremiah E. Rankin

"Let There Be Peace on Earth" by Sy Miller and Jill Jackson

"Sent Out in Jesus' Name," Trad. Cuban

"Amen," Trad. Gospel

"Pass It On" by Kurt Kaiser

RESOURCE
GROUP COVENANT TEMPLATE

We covenant together to deal with our differences in a spirit of mutual respect and to refrain from actions that may harm the emotional and physical well-being of others.

The following principles will guide our actions:

- We will treat others whose views may differ from our own with the same courtesy we would want to receive ourselves.
- We will listen with a sincere desire to understand the point of view being expressed by another person, especially if it is different from our own.
- We will respect one another's ideas, feelings, and experiences.
- We will refrain from blaming or judging in our attitude and behavior toward others.
- We will communicate directly in a respectful and constructive way with any person with whom we may disagree.
- We will seek feedback to ensure that we have truly understood one another in our communications.
- We will maintain confidentiality.

Additional agreements for our particular group:

FINAL EVALUATION
GROUP LEADER

Church or Group Name

Location   Group Leader

....

Volume (Check One)   ☐ Priorities   ☐ Respect   ☐ Relationship   ☐ Truth

Group Composition   Total Registered   _____
                               Total Finished   _____
                               Racial / Ethnic Composition (optional):

                               [   ]

Did any who did not finish the study leave because they were not enjoying the group?

☐ Yes   ☐ No

If yes, do you know why?

[   ]

To what extent was there a diversity of opinion in the group?

☐ All the time   ☐ Some of the time   ☐ Not much at all

Think back over all the reading and group experiences in light of the following questions. On a scale of 1–10, how much do you agree with the following statements:

1 = Strongly disagree
10 = Strongly agree

The group engaged the discussions with respect for differing views. _____
Participants came to group sessions prepared. _____
I ran into issues I did not feel prepared to handle. _____
We experienced conflict that made some participants quit. _____
The issues we discussed were relevant to the group. _____
The material was easy to follow. _____
All participants were willing to express opinions. _____
We had members who repeatedly did not adhere to the group covenant. _____
The participants knew one another well before joining this group. _____
I believe everyone was being honest with one another. _____
We were able to cover the topics within the timeframe. _____
The discussion questions were helpful. _____

Other comments:

FINAL EVALUATION
PARTICIPANT

_____
Church or Group Name

_____ _____
Location   Group Leader

Think back over all the reading and group experiences in light of the following questions. On a scale of 1–10, how much do you agree with the following statements:

1 = Strongly disagree
10 = Strongly agree

I learned something new.	_____
I feel more able to talk about social issues than when I began.	_____
This has been a positive experience for me.	_____
I now understand the other side of some issues differently.	_____
Those in my group were open and honest with their opinions.	_____
Those in my group were respectful of one another.	_____
The reading material presented issues fairly.	_____
I typically share my opinions with others.	_____
I enjoyed the exercises in our group sessions.	_____
I felt unable to express my opinions in our group.	_____
The exercises made it safer to express my opinions and ideas.	_____
I enjoyed the reading.	_____
We covered important issues.	_____

Other comments:

_____
_____
_____
_____
_____
_____

Add me to your email list: _____

Other comments:

RESOURCE
ADVERTISING HELPS

All groups are free to advertise for members as they see fit, but if you'd like some help in describing what it is people are signing up for, you are free to copy or adapt the following:

EXPLORING JUSTICE: THE TEN COMMANDMENTS

Have you ever wondered how we got to be so divided? Do you long for a place where you could explore social issues in a respectful environment? Then join us for six weeks to study Priorities, the first volume in a new series that examines social justice issues through the lens of the Ten Commandments. No matter what side of the issues you're on, you'll be able to express your opinions, listen to others, and learn the history behind some of our deepest divisions.

This first study focuses on the opening commandments to have no other gods, make no idols, and refrain from taking God's name in vain. By looking at how modern idols fuel our divisions and stall justice, we'll explore protests, issues surrounding the flag, pledge of allegiance, and national anthem, the First and Second Amendments, tearing down monuments, nationalism, "America First," and more.

[Here you should put the specifics of when and where the group will meet and for how long, who is leading it, cost of the book (and how to obtain it), and who to call with questions or to register. You can download the series logo and/or the book cover to use in your advertising here: massbible.org/priorities-ad-helps]

www.ingramcontent.com/pod-product-compliance
Lightning Source LLC
Chambersburg PA
CBHW080446110426
42743CB00016B/3299